UNCENSORED

UNCENSORED

FINDING GOD WHEN HE FEELS FAR AWAY

JEANNE MAYO

HIGHERLIFE DEVELOPMENT SERVICES
OVIEDO, FLORIDA

09 10 11 12 13 – 8 7 6 5 4 3 2 1

UNCENSORED: Finding God When He Feels Far Away
ISBN 13: 978-1-935245-02-5
ISBN 10: 1-9352450-2-3
Copyright © 2009 by Jeanne Mayo
P.O. Box 450309
Atlanta, Georgia 31145

Published by HigherLife Press
2342 Westminster Terrace
Oviedo, Florida 32765
407-563-4806
www.ahigherlife.com

Printed in the United States of America

FOR THOSE WHO DARE TO ASK
THE TOUGH QUESTIONS

THANKS

To my treasured Elijah who has made me a "Nana" and made my heart burst with more love than I ever dreamed possible. May you forever be a "man after God's own heart" and one who follows Christ wholeheartedly...even through the dark and lonely seasons.

Your Nana prays for you more often than you'll probably ever realize. Let's go to Disney World together!

To my hero, Sam, as well as Josh, Monica, and Justin, for being the greatest "fam" in the universe.

To Mike and Diane Rogers...for believing in the dream of ministry multiplication and courageously blazing a path with me. Your friendship means more than words could ever reflect on this piece of paper. True friends, like I often say to you, are so very rare. You have earned that title in a million meaningful ways. Here's to a long journey of significant friendship, helicopter rides, redneck jokes, and fishing t-shirts!

To Mitch and Christine Soule...who miraculously entered my life and allowed me to deeply adopt you into my heart. You have captured my love by your sensitive unselfishness and blazing Christ-likeness. Thank you for the honor, Christine, of being in the hospital room that day. It is my honor to be your other "mom." And thank you, Mitch, for being such a great dad that I often hear your voice break when you speak of your children.

To My Adopted Sister Barbara Hardcastle...for filling the "big sis" crevice in such a deep and steadying way. It is so natural to pick the phone up and say, "Please pray." I trust you know what a rare and priceless gift you are to me. We began the journey together as I loved on your grandchildren. Now you are loving on thousands of other people's grandchildren through Youth Leader's Coach. What a miracle of multiplication.

To Dan and Megan Valentine...who have anchored my heart by your moments of costly love and personal commitment. Words are cheap when I try to tell you how proud I am of all you are now doing for the Kingdom. Thank you, too, for the constancy of your friendship, through both the good and the challenging times. I celebrate deeply this next chapter of your lives. Just remember that I will always, always be in your corner.

To Lee and Janie Horner, for helping me believe that genuine friendship roots can last for 30 years and only deepen. Your continual "watching after us" makes my heart safe now in many deep ways, and your "let's take care of this" attitude makes me feel secure as I glance ahead. And now, thank you for allowing Jon and Gina to be part of the Cadre. History repeats itself...in loving and unforgettable ways. We are blessed families of legacy and love.

To my deeply respected son in the Lord, Ray Archer...who has walked through more fire than most people will ever know. You, of all people, understand the underlying theme of this book— dealing with the times when God feels far away and when the loneliness reverberates. Claudia awaits you in heaven, my son. And she has two perfect legs now. You'll take long, loving walks together. But until then, we'll continue to live a life of relentless faith in the One we call "Lord."

To Rufus and Berna Oladapo...for becoming so much more than just "members of our congregation"—but trusted members of our hearts. Without your sacrifice and love, countless lives in Atlanta and through Master's Commission never would have been reached. But even more, thank you for the friendship moments. Our lives are so much richer because of text messages from the hospital waiting room and dinners together at Ruby Tuesday.

To my publishing gifts at HIGHER LIFE...Most especially David Welday, but also to Marsha McCoy, Carey Huffman, Eric Powell, Cathleen Kwas, and Valerie Kosky...only you know all the extra hours invested into this project to make its unveiling possible at my upcoming National Youth Leader's Conference. I am so deeply grateful that you allowed me to partner with you. Thank you for going so very, very far beyond the norm. I am eternally indebted to you.

And last but never least...to my most treasured Youth Leader's Coach team...Judy Gregory, Bethany Shay, Alisha Ramirez, Josh Mayo, Chris Infalt, Brett Bishop, Jay Parmenter, Sterling Rowan, and the one and only Jordan Marcon...for giving me the privilege of "doing life" with my best friends. Just last evening, most of you were up late, helping to pull off another miraculous NYLC. And then even later into the night, we were still laughing, brewing fresh coffee, and drawing crazy stick figures inside this manuscript. What memories! May we celebrate purpose, ministry, and life together for many more fulfilling years to come. *Life really is found in giving life away...TOGETHER.*

World's Best Team

Table of Contents

WARNING! → In your face reality ahead!

FEELING close to God and BEING close to God are two really different things.

Get this one!

01

HIDE AND SEEK

So here's the ugly truth: I don't **feel God** a lot of the time. In fact, sometimes I feel like He's playing a pretty tricky game of hide and seek with me. How about you?

Sadly, people in the church world never seem to talk about those confusing times. You know, those times of suffocating silence when it feels like God is nowhere to be found. The times when you try to pray, but it seems like you're just talking to the ceiling. Some people think an angel is supposed to show up every time they start to read the Bible. That's crazy!

Let me tell you part of my own story. I came to have a personal relationship with Christ as a teenager. When I was growing up, my family wasn't exactly "Leave It to Beaver," so I wanted a dad I was close to more than words could express. The night I officially gave my life to Christ, I truly "felt" my heavenly Father in an incredible way. I guess I just assumed that the warm, fuzzy feelings would hang around. Not so. Like nearly everything else in life, extraordinary feelings (both natural and spiritual) come and go.

Ministers didn't help my problem much. They would say things on Sunday like, "I just *sense* the presence of the Lord here today." As for me, I guess my "sensor" was broken, because I usually sensed nothing (except the fact I was ready for lunch). There was even a sweet, old saint in my church (with a pretty direct line to God) who often proclaimed, "If you can't *feel* the Lord today in this service, then you're already dead!" Yet another problem. Not only was my spiritual "sensor" broken, but now I was officially *dead*. Not a good day in anyone's book.

RIP

What I didn't realize then was that all the great heroes of faith have experienced times like this. C.S. Lewis called it "The Whirlpool State." Mother Theresa called it "The

Even the Big Dawgs

Silent Years." And Billy Graham talks about when God "lifts His conscious presence." You see, the Word of God makes it clear that if we follow Christ, <u>God never, ever leaves us.</u> But, for a lot of different reasons, our *conscious awareness* of His presence can be blocked from time to time. For instance, my husband might be in a different room of our home. Even though I may not be *aware* of his presence, that doesn't mean he's not there. In the same way, sometimes God removes our *consciousness of His presence—but never His actual presence.*

I will NEVER leave you.
– God

NOT ONLY WAS MY SPIRITUAL "SENSOR" BROKEN, BUT NOW I WAS OFFICIALLY *DEAD*.

So this huge important dilemma is why I decided to write this book. I want to help other sincere, but sometimes confused people like me, understand what's really going on when God feels a million miles away. <u>I want to help you</u> understand the freeing reality that <u>"*feeling close to God*" and "*being close to God*" are two really *different things*.</u>

So grab a Dr Pepper or a good cup of coffee, and let's begin our journey together. I promise you, my friend, that the trip will be both freeing and life-changing. How do I know? Because <u>I wish someone would have taken me on this journey many years ago.</u> It's my prayer that some of my honest insights can spare you some of the confusion and heartache I experienced.

Amen :)

By the way, thanks for picking up this book. I prayed **(That's you!)** that the right people would find it. At the risk of sounding cheesy, this must be a "God-appointment" for us. So, let's get started!

Bang!

So grab a
Dr Pepper or
a good cup of
coffee, and
let's begin our
journey together.

Shhhh

The teacher
doesn't talk
while giving the
test.

Chapter

02

NO TOUCH REQUIRED

Now I don't know about you, but my favorite part of school was never the tests. As a matter of fact, I could have done without them entirely! But when I began to sort through the times when I felt like God was really far away, I remembered something about those test experiences that actually helped me out. That is, *the teacher seldom talked while giving a test.* Interesting. I wonder if that has anything to do with some of God's silent times in my life?

Especially Mrs. Stroud— 2nd grade reading teacher

    Years ago, I heard a guy tell about a dream he had. <u>That dream had a life-changing impact on me.</u> Even more, it helped me understand what was really going on during those times when it feels like God is a million miles away.

8

Let me share it with you from the vantage point of the guy who had the experience.

"In my dream, I saw three young men praying. It was obvious that all three of them were for real in their attempts to grow closer to Christ. So while they were praying, without their realizing it, Jesus appeared directly behind them. He stopped to listen to what each of them was saying. Then Jesus began to relate to each young man individually.

1st Guy ↓

"He came closer to the first guy and listened to his prayer. Then Jesus walked around and stood in front of the guy, talking face-to-face and making sure the young man felt deeply heard and understood. After a few more moments of personal interaction, Jesus embraced the guy, and then disappeared. What a prayer time this guy had that memorable morning!

2nd Guy ↓

"As the dream continued, Jesus then went to the second person who was praying. Christ stood behind him and listened intently to his prayer. Eventually, He came closer to the young man and gave him a pat on the back. It seemed that Jesus wanted to assure the guy that He was really there. Then, without any personal conversation, Jesus stepped away and continued to listen quietly from the background. As a matter of fact, there was no face-to-face exchange or embrace between the two. Jesus gave this second guy only a brief touch. Moments later, Jesus again disappeared quietly. Strange, I thought to myself. But at least he had direct contact with Jesus—even if only for a moment.

"In the dream's final sequence, Jesus appeared behind a third guy who was praying. But this time, Christ seemed more distant and removed. He listened to every word the young man was saying, yet He never made any form of physical contact. There was no embrace, no pat on the back, no friendly squeeze of the arm, and no face-to-face connection. After listening to the third guy's prayer for several minutes, Jesus again disappeared. Wow! Not exactly 'up close and personal,' I thought.

"At this point, I was pretty confused, yet eager to ask the Lord a few questions of my own. So I said, 'Father, help me understand what I just saw. All three young men sincerely wanted to grow in their relationship with You. I want to know what the first **#1** guy did that made him so close to You. I mean, You listened and talked with him face-to-face. Help me understand his secrets, so I can have a relationship with you that's as close as this guy had.'

"'But the two other guys who were praying, help me understand them too, Jesus,' I continued. 'The second **#2** man seemed pretty tight with You, Lord. After all, You touched him briefly. But then there was the third **#3** man. I don't ever want there to be that kind of distance between You and me!'

> SOMETIMES
> THEIR EMOTIONAL
> ADDICTIONS LEAVE
> ME FEELING REALLY,
> REALLY LONELY.
> —GOD

"The Lord paused before answering me. His eyes were filled with gentle compassion and fatherly love. 'You have it all wrong,' He answered.

"'The first young man is very new in his faith and has known Me for only a short while. I knew that unless he *felt Me* as he prayed, he would be too weak to continue in his relationship with Me. The second young man is more mature. We have become closer. He no longer totally depends on his feelings to trust My reality. So he doesn't need to feel Me quite as much to know that I'm listening when he prays.'

3rd
Guy

"'But the third young man,' Jesus concluded, 'he is the one who has most captured My heart. You see, he has grown deep in his faith. His walk with Me is not based on shallow, human feelings. Instead, his trust is based on My Word. Even when feelings are nonexistent, his pursuit of Me remains the same. That's why I can depend on him. Whether he feels My presence or not, I can trust him to follow Me faithfully. That's why this third young man is the one who honors Me most.'

Faith

"Jesus paused once again. I heard a tinge of sadness in His voice as He said one last thing in the dream: 'I only wish more of My children would base their relationship with Me around My Word instead of around their feelings. Sometimes their emotional addictions leave Me feeling really, really lonely.'"

God to
you

NO TOUCH REQUIRED

So here's the bottom line. All of us love the luxury of "good feelings"—even in our walk with Christ. But it takes no character or maturity to follow Him when experiencing all sorts of spiritual sensations and goose bumps. If you want to rank up there among Christ's most trusted friends, base your relationship with Him around His Word, not your feelings. And someday quietly tell Him, "*I'm growing up in You, Lord. No touch required.*"

"What you do speaks so loud I cannot hear what you say."

— Emerson

Before any picture can be developed, it has to go through the dark room.

Chapter

03

THE DARK ROOM

"**Lord, help me *grow*** in You. Help me *develop* into all You
created me to be." Ever said something like that to God?
I have. I didn't realize that one of the Lord's greatest ways
to strengthen me spiritually is to take me through some of
those dark, unfeeling times in my relationship with Him.
You don't have to be a photographer to know that *before any
picture can be developed, it has to go through the dark room.* If you're
serious about "spiritual development," expect to face some
dark, tough times along the way.

Not fun, but true

    All true champions know that pain is part of the process,
but it eventually passes. *Pain is simply the passageway to promotion.*
So let's look at five positive reasons why God might
allow you to go through times when you feel distant and

15

Don't cheat!

detached from Him. It's a course requirement if you enroll in "Spiritual Growth University." As you consider these possibilities, pause after each one to figure out if that might be part of what you're going through. The "self-help" questions at the end of each point might help.

01. God wants to help you actually grow in love *with Him*—rather than in love with the *feelings of Him*. It's easy to begin "worshiping your feelings" more than really worshiping the Lord Himself.

So sometimes the Father wisely allows spiritual *feelings* to be blocked so we can build our faith around *Him—not around our feelings and emotions.* These times can get pretty confusing though because when we're *"feeling God,"* it's really easy to believe that we love Him more. But at these times, do we really love *the Lord more*, or do we love *the feelings more*?

> WHEN YOU KNOW AND LOVE A PERSON DEEPLY, YOU'RE COMFORTABLE WITH PERIODS OF SILENCE.

In every relationship, feelings come and go. It's the same in your spiritual life. I've been married to my amazing husband for a lot of great years, but I don't freak out during the normal seasons when I don't "feel" particularly mushy and romantic. I've even learned that when you know and love a person deeply, you're comfortable with periods of silence. If that's all true in human relationships, I think we can expect it in our most treasured spiritual one. Again, *God wants us to fall in love with Him — rather than in love with feelings of Him.* How are you doing on this one?

Be honest...

[ ]   Ouch—I needed to hear this one!

[ ]   Nope—Feelings aren't a big deal to me.

02. **God wants you to take His crash course on spiritual growth and maturity in order to develop deep spiritual roots.** Have you ever noticed that trees growing close to a river are easily uprooted by storms? That's because the roots of those trees never have to go very deep into the ground. As long as the water is easily reached, the roots remain really shallow.

It works the same way with people. For our spiritual roots to grow deep in the soil of God's Word, we have to go through some "dry times." While wandering these spiritual deserts, God will often feel countless miles away. He's not playing a cruel game of "hide and seek." Instead, He's creating circumstances that will bring strength and depth to your spiritual roots. He doesn't want you to get "blown away" when the next storm comes to your life.

Have you ever been mountain climbing? If so, you know that the *higher* you climb, the *thinner* the air gets. *Only deeply rooted things grow high up on the mountains.* So if you want to get some "spiritual elevation," I think this is all part of the deal.

[ ]   Come to think of it, my "roots" are getting deeper, and I like that!

[ ]   Sorry. I'm OK with where my roots are now.

03.   **God wants to cultivate a naked dependence on His Word as your basis of faith. He wants to forever**

separate in your mind "spiritual *feelings*" from "spiritual reality." It's easy to have unrealistic expectations of spiritual feelings in your walk with Christ. I mean, angels don't show up every time you break out your Bible or start to pray. The whole Christian life is based on your *faith*—not your *feelings.* Isn't it interesting that "feelings" are rarely even talked about in the Bible? **Nowhere in the Word are "spiritual feelings" ever equated to "spiritual reality."** (Go back and re-read that last sentence to make sure you really get it. I think it's a "big deal" statement.)

Big reality check— don't miss it!

Jesus knows that our feelings are inconsistent, and that true, lasting faith comes only as we develop authentic trust in His Word. So sometimes He will wisely block our "feeling level" so we will be forced to cultivate deeper dependence on His Word. But smile. Just because you don't feel anything doesn't mean that nothing is happening. If you've ever done weight training, you know that after most workouts, you don't *feel* like anything has actually happened—except that you're really tired and you actually feel weaker for a while. But your feelings are very different from the reality of what is developing inside you. So what am I trying to say? This same thing is true when it comes to building spiritual muscles. So keep "lifting," even when it doesn't feel very good.

[ ]   Yeah, I depend on His Word as my basis of faith even when I don't "feel" God.

[ ]   No, when I'm tired of "heavy lifting," I just stop reading the Bible until the feelings come back.

04.   **God wisely realizes that too much "spiritual light" isn't good for you. So sometimes He allows non-feeling times for your own spiritual health and protection.** Yes, spiritual "dark times" come to all of us. The Lord realizes that we can't stand constant spiritual (or physical) light. If the power were always on, we'd "blow our circuits." Even our physical body shows our need

IF SATAN CAN'T MESS YOU UP ANY OTHER WAY, HE'LL TRY THE "NO FEELINGS MEANS NO FAITH" TRICK.

for darkness in our nightly sleep patterns. Research has shown that certain disease-fighting processes require not just rest, but dark downtimes to function at peak levels. So, spiritual "dark times" can be our friends if we understand what's going on. It's really common for such a time to come right after we've had a lot of spiritual light and truth. The darkness is God's loving way of giving us time to deeply grasp the truth we've already received. He doesn't want us to "over-amp," blow our emotional circuits and have a spiritual power failure.

[ ] This stinks but I can be OK with having some dark times if it is for my own good.

[ ] You're on drugs, Jeanne. Dark times stink, and I'm not signing up for them.

05. Congratulations—The devil might hate your guts!

If you're an athlete, you know that the opponent typically tries to take out the strongest, best players on the opposing team—the ones with the most potential to "score." So realize that if Satan can't mess you up any other way, he'll try the "no feelings means no faith" trick. I'm sure it's included in Satan's "Warfare Tactics 101 Manual." So as strange as it sounds, maybe you should regard your dark, dry season as a backhanded compliment from the devil. You're valuable enough to God's kingdom that the enemy wants to take you out. So congrats! Maybe Satan realizes the great plans and destiny Christ has ahead for you—and he's just plain *scared* of you.

> [] Wow! My favorite one. Hope the devil is scared of me!
>
> [] Are you kidding? I am not spiritual enough to be on his hit list.

I realize that those five possibilities aren't always *great fun*, but they really do produce **great growth**. The Iroquois Indians had an age-old custom that might help you better understand the Father's purpose during dark and "silent" times. It happened whenever a young boy in the tribe was initiated into manhood. Let me share it with you. I think it relates to the "dark room" times we all experience as we grow and mature in our walks with Christ.

When an Iroquois boy reached the age of 12, he would be led out, at night, into the darkest and most dangerous part of the forest. The boy had to spend the night by himself, with no weapon or anyone to protect him. The darkness was so intense that even the moon was hidden. If he successfully stood guard for the entire night, the tribesmen would return in the morning and honor the boy as a true man. But if the darkness became too frightening, and he ran back to the village, his promotion to manhood was postponed indefinitely.

Picture the scene. The young boy would sit on the ground, naked and alone, watching the torches of the adult tribesmen fade into the black forest. Then, shivering in cold isolation, he began the battle with his imagination. Every sound made him jump, fearing that a wild animal was about to leap from the darkness and tear him limb from limb. Sleep eluded him as the shroud of night concealed disaster that could strike at any moment. A thousand voices inside his head must have told him to run back to the light and safety of the village.

Hours later, if the boy courageously outlasted the darkness, the morning light would begin to break. The young boy would blink, rub his eyes and wearily welcome the dawn. Squinting to survey his surroundings, his eyes would catch sight of a large figure concealed in the high trees just behind him. There, quietly positioned in a nearby tree, was a sight that instantly brought confidence and relief to the frightened young man. Without the boy knowing it,

his father had spent the entire night there in the forest with him—his arrow drawn and ready to defend his son from any harm. At the first sign of danger, his father would have come out of the darkness to protect the boy with his own life. The loving father would have never allowed his son to face the darkness alone. But in order to grow and mature, the boy had to choose to conquer his fears and confusion. Though he may have felt abandoned and forgotten, his feelings were lies. He was under his father's protection the whole time. As the father watched, the boy's courage outlasted the night. When the daylight finally scattered the darkness that next morning, it revealed a young boy who was maturing into true manhood.

I think all of us see the parallels. We want to mature just like the young boy, except we want to mature into spiritual adulthood. But sometimes the price is costly and leaves us feeling all alone. So how about all those prayers you've prayed? You know, the ones about wanting to grow in God. Maybe God is using some of the "spiritually dark times" to develop your character and answer those prayers. Just remember that no matter how dark and deserted you feel, God is always right there. Next time, try glancing up in a nearby tree. You never know Who you might see!

Thank God!

You're not
finished just
because you sin;
you're finished
if you choose to
quit.

04

HIS SILENCE = YOUR FAULT

Check the cover. We called this book "Uncensored." So let

There's that word again!

me be blunt and straight with you. Sometimes God feels

far away because of stupid (choices) we've made. Granted,

sometimes the Lord engineers some of these "non-feeling

times" for our spiritual growth. Other times, however, we

bring them on ourselves. So if it seems that God is far away,

try going back to where you "left Him." Let me point out

six common mistakes (i.e., stupid choices) that can make it

feel like God is really, really far away. But take heart! It's not

the end of the world when you mess up. You see, you're not

finished just because you sin; you're finished if you choose

to quit. I've included some more self-help questions to help you figure out which choices you've been making—and which ones you might want to change.

01. **Sometimes we feel far away from God because we've invested little or no effort in our friendship with Him.**

This is my problem 50% of the time

I mean, if we go for several days (or weeks) without praying or reading God's Word, we're probably going to start feeling pretty distant from Him. It may seem that God has pulled away, but your own spiritual laziness is probably the problem. Think about what happens in our human relationships when we don't take time to connect and hang out with each other. We grow distant. When it comes to a God we can't see—and often don't feel—how much more do we need to make a deliberate effort to stay connected to Him through times in His Word and prayer? If our devotion to God becomes dependent on our feelings, we'll never develop the discipline to make it through tough times—let alone accomplish God's ultimate purpose for our lives.

[ ]   Sadly, I can relate. I haven't spent time with
        God ... in a while. Maybe I should start.

[ ]   Nope, I'm pretty consistent with my time in the
        Word and in prayer.

02.   **Sometimes we feel far from God because of our own**
      willful choices to disobey Him and His Word. At these

times, we create our own distance from God and

separate ourselves from Him.
Let me give you an example.
Throughout many years in the
ministry, I've seen awesome
Christian young adults begin to
get romantically involved with
nonbelievers. (The Bible says
that this is a "no-go.") Days,
weeks, or months later, they
tell me, "I just can't feel God
anymore." Let me help you understand what's really
happening here.

> **IF OUR DEVOTION TO GOD BECOMES DEPENDENT ON OUR FEELINGS, WE'LL NEVER DEVELOP THE DISCIPLINE TO MAKE IT THROUGH TOUGH TIMES.**

Don't let this be you...

If you choose to ignore God's voice and guidance in certain areas of life (i.e. relationships), His voice (and presence) begins to get softer and softer. The longer you refuse to obey Him, the softer His voice becomes. The more you ignore the tug of His Spirit on your conscience, the less you'll feel that tug. Remember—the Holy Spirit is a gentleman. He won't push Himself on anyone who doesn't want Him. Eventually, it may seem like God is not only silent, but nowhere to be found. What's really happening is that a persistent choice to disobey has "plugged your spiritual ears."

Disobedience = Distance

Need another example? Spend several hours exploring porn on the Internet, and you probably won't feel Jesus hanging out to watch it with you! It's the same thing when we allow resentment and unforgiveness to grow inside our hearts. We begin to feel very far from God. But once again, our willful choices to disobey His Word have created the distance.

[] Hmmm, I can think of some choices I've made recently that would move me away from God.

[] Nobody's perfect, but overall, I've been making the right choices. Good for me!

03. **Other times, God feels far away when we're going through a time of physical and/or emotional drain. We don't have energy left for anything—including feeling God.** It was Charles Spurgeon who said, "When fatigue walks in, faith walks out." Times of heavy emotional strain or drain can do the same thing to us. Don't mistake these times as "sin." You just need to take some time for your physical and/or emotional "energy battery" to re-charge.

So true

THE LONGER YOU REFUSE TO OBEY HIM, THE SOFTER HIS VOICE BECOMES. THE MORE YOU IGNORE THE TUG OF HIS SPIRIT ON YOUR CONSCIENCE, THE LESS YOU'LL FEEL THAT TUG.

Sometimes, the most spiritual thing you can do is rest (not an excuse for laziness). So slow down a little and *zzzzz...*

get some decent sleep. You might be surprised how much closer you feel to God in a few days.

> [ ]   That's me! Maybe I do need to get a little more rest.
>
> [ ]   Probably not. Me and my snooze button are already good friends!

04.   Sometimes life takes some painful, rotten turns. Bad things really do happen to good people. At moments when we are deeply hurt and life doesn't make sense, it's easy for the pain to make us feel far away from God. Internally, it's easy to get pretty angry with Him. Everything inside of us screams "Why?" The good news is that He understands your emotions and is strong enough to handle our pain, confusion, and junk—even our occasional outbursts. But here's the bad news: These feelings—if allowed to take control—can build a wall between the Lord and us, creating a sense of distance from the Father at the very moment we most need Him to be close to us.

Re-read this one—you can't afford not to get it.

Now let me be really clear on something: Having painful, negative emotions after a tragedy is **NOT sin.** We all experience times when it feels like our whole world has been turned upside down. Anger, pain, frustration—even questions about our faith—are part of the package. The problem comes, though, when we continue to rehearse those negative feelings over and over in our minds for many months after the event. We let the "WHYs?" scream so loudly in our heads that we don't honestly try to sort through the emotional baggage. We keep fanning the flames of frustration and allowing the emotional garbage to pile up instead of slowly beginning the process of healing. It's almost as though we **want** resentment and doubt to take up permanent residence inside our hearts. When that happens, we create a barrier between ourselves and the Lord. As a result, we isolate ourselves from Him at the very moment He most wants be close to us and take care of us.

After facing a few major tragedies in my life, I've come to believe that some things will never make sense to my human mind until I reach heaven. Deuteronomy 29:29 says, "There are *secret things* that belong only to the Lord our God...but the revealed things belong to us." So when I experience some of the "secret things" that I really can't understand, I've learned to *run towards God* with my hurt, confusion, and anger—instead of *running away from Him*. It keeps the walls down and my internal peace up.

[ ] Ouch, but wow. I've allowed the pain to build a wall between me and the Lord.

[ ] Not so much. I've tried to let those rotten turns push me toward the Lord.

05. I often say, "Show me your friends and I'll show you your future." This principle impacts your ability to "feel God," too. When you spend too much time hanging out with nonbelievers or people who are half-hearted in their faith, you'll slowly begin to adopt their attitudes and their way of thinking. Distance between

Seldom want to admit— but so true.

you and the Lord will become inevitable. On the other hand, staying involved with church and hanging out with good, godly friends can make a big, positive difference. Remember this: Your friends are like the buttons on an elevator. They either bring you up — or take you down.

> [] I hate admitting it, but I think my friendship choices could be part of the problem.
>
> [] My closest friends really do help me want to know God more — not less.

06. **Guilt can block your ability to feel close to God.** If you try to live with "one foot in the world and the other foot in His Kingdom," the two worlds will eventually collide. At that point, you must make a heavy-duty decision regarding which world you're going to live in. If you think you can wait to make the decision, you've already decided. And the guilt will continue to block your closeness to God. There is only one way to get rid of the guilt. Remember our earlier quote? "When

you feel like God is far away, try going back to where you left Him."

On the other hand, watch out for the flip side of this one, too. *Once you've sincerely asked the Lord for His forgiveness on something, don't let the enemy haunt you with false guilt.* You can't *earn* Christ's forgiveness any more than you can *earn* the sacrifice He made through His death on the cross. Satan will try to hang guilt over your head for as long as you allow. That's why he's described in the Bible as "The Accuser of those of faith."

[] When I'm honest with myself, I do feel guilty … and I know why.

[] I've already asked for forgiveness; now I just need to believe that I'm forgiven.

[] Text message the world! Finally one I don't relate to!

Let me be clear. I've created my own silence with the Lord—in each of these categories—on more occasions than I want to admit. But when I mess up, God's pursuing (love) keeps chasing after me. I'm reminded of a true story I heard, which took place in California a few years back.

Thousands of cars are stolen every year in California. Strangely enough, one car theft made the headlines in several local papers. It was even the lead story on the evening news. The police issued an all-points bulletin to find the missing car and the person who stole it. They tried to persuade the thief to turn himself in to the authorities.

Why was this particular theft getting so much attention? Let me give you the [rest of the story.]

WHEN YOU FEEL LIKE GOD IS FAR AWAY, TRY GOING BACK TO WHERE YOU LEFT HIM.

The owner of the stolen car had told police that on the front seat was a box of innocent looking crackers that had been laced with a deadly poison. He had planned to use the crackers as bait to kill some wild animals that were destroying his farm property. So you see, the police were desperately trying to find the thief—*not to punish him,*

BUT TO SAVE HIS LIFE. They were afraid he would eat one of the crackers and die before help could reach him.

It's the same way between you and Jesus, maybe even as you read this chapter. His truth is pursuing you—<u>NOT</u> because He wants to <u>*punish*</u> you—but because He wants to <u>*save*</u> <u>you</u>. When you break God's law and create your own "darkness" and distance from God, He lovingly pursues you. He's trying to *rescue* you, not *condemn* you. Flip back through the pages and look at your answers. If any of those points apply to you, why not take a few minutes right now and talk to Him about it?

And if you're running from God, I plead with you—*for your own good*—*stop running, and "turn yourself in." Your spiritual life may be at stake.*

"I count the man braver who overcomes his desires than the man who conquers his enemies. For the hardest victory in the universe is the VICTORY OVER SELF."
-Aristotle

"God never consults your PAST to create your FUTURE."

Chapter 05

VOICES FROM THE ROOM OF SHADOWS

Yes, sometimes we all create our own spiritual "darkness" and "silence" by stupid choices and selfish desires. But before we go any further, let me give you a huge dose of HOPE about facing your own sins honestly. You see, nothing will make God feel further away from you than the Enemy's haunting reminders about all the places in life you've miserably failed. I know. I can't tell you how many times Satan has whispered into my head, reminding me of my sins—both big and small. And unfortunately, long after the Lord has forgiven them, the Enemy keeps reminding me about them. I've learned that Satan will keep talking to me as long as I will keep listening.

? ? ?

So how do you deal with the voices of guilt that keep screaming in your mind? You know, the ones that make God feel like He's a million miles away. The ones that tell you that He's not listening to you anymore. The ones that say you don't *deserve* to be close to the Living God because of what you've done. The ones that come when God's voice feels non-existent and every attempt to pray seems like a big joke.

Someone is reading my mind

I SAW A WHOLE WALL OF THE ROOM THAT WAS COVERED WITH SMALL INDEX-CARD FILES.

Years ago, I heard a guy named Joshua Harris share on these pretty agonizing seasons. He's a writer and a speaker who talks a lot about relationships. He related a story from a dream he had that relates to these guilt-filled dark times. Let me try to recount most of his words. If you're the less-than-perfect person that I am, I think it will mean a lot to you. And because we're talking about the times when God feels far away because of our sin and guilt, let me call his dream, "Voices from the Room of Shadows."

I found myself in that place between being awake and still dreaming. Weird as it was, **I was in a huge room.** It was a really dark room. Really, really dark. There were shadows all around. The shadows were so thick that I could barely see through them. I rubbed my eyes in the dream and tried to focus on the surroundings. Through the darkness, I could only see one thing. It was a **whole wall of the room that was covered with small index-card files.**

The cards were like the ones you see in libraries where titles and authors are listed in alphabetical order. But these files, which somehow stretched from the floor to the ceiling, looked like they were endless. They also seemed to have different headings on them. As I drew closer to the wall of files, the first one that grabbed my attention was labeled, "Girls I Have Liked." I opened it and began to flip through all the cards. I quickly shut the drawer because I recognized all the names written on the cards.

Then, somehow I knew in an instant what I was looking at. I was standing in front of a **catalogue system of my entire life!** On each of these countless cards were written

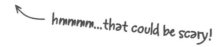
hmmmm...that could be scary!

actions of every moment of my life, both big and small. I was blown away by what I was seeing.

My life in here

I had a sense of joy as I looked at some of the files. There was one called "Friends" that brought back so many great memories. But next to it, my eyes fell on a drawer labeled "Friends I Have Betrayed." My shame and regret were so huge that I glanced nervously over my shoulder to make sure no one was looking.

There were all sorts of other titles that ranged from the mundane to the weird: "Books I Have Read," "Lies I Have Told," even "Jokes I Have Laughed At." Some of the files were pretty funny. But many of them were agonizing in their accuracy and their data. Often there were more cards than I expected to find in a file. Sometimes, though, there were fewer than I hoped.

Was it possible that after living only twenty years that I had written these millions of cards? Yet, as I glanced at separate cards throughout the collection, they all verified their truthfulness. Each card was clearly written in my

own handwriting. Each one was even signed with my own
haunting signature. X *John Hancock*

When I pulled out the file marked, "Songs I Have
Listened To," I realized that the files apparently grew over
time to contain even the most recent contents. The cards
in this file were packed really tightly together. After two or
three yards of cabinets, I still hadn't found the end of the
file. I finally shut the drawer, not shamed so much by the
quality of the music, but more by the huge amount of time I
knew that file represented.

Then I came to a file marked "Lustful Thoughts." At
that instant, I felt a chill run through my body. I pulled out
the file only an inch, not wanting to test its size and then
pulled out one of its cards. I shuddered at how detailed and
accurate its contents were. I felt sick and humiliated that
such a moment was actually recorded.

That's a file I wish I could make disappear...

Suddenly, I felt an almost overpowering rage inside
myself. One key thought screamed out in my mind: "No
one must ever see these cards! I have to destroy all of them!"

So in an almost insane panic, I tried to yank the file out. No matter how heavy or long it was, I knew the contents just had to be destroyed. But as I took the file at one end and tried to pound it against the floor, a painful reality became immediately clear: **I could not dislodge even one single card. Nor could I tear the cards apart. They seemed as strong as steel.**

I finally melted to the floor, feeling helpless and defeated. I fought the urge to cry like a little kid. In my desperation, I let out a long, painful sigh. But then, to make matters even worse, my eyes fell on another file. It was entitled, "People I Have Shared the Gospel With." The handle was brighter than those around it, newer, almost unused. I pulled on it and a small box, not more than three inches long, fell into my hands. With embarrassment, I could easily count the handful of cards it contained. 1, 2, 3, 4...

An eye-opening reality

I couldn't take any more. The tears began to flow. Sobs came from deep inside myself, so deep that the hurt started in my stomach and then echoed through my whole body. I fell on my knees and cried in deep shame. Almost taunting me, the rows of file shelves swirled in front of my tear-filled eyes. No one must ever, ever see this room. I must find a way to lock it up and hide the key.

But then, at the depth of my anguish, I saw HIM. Everything inside of me stood still.

"No please, not Him! Not here!" my thoughts screamed out on the inside. "Oh, God, please let this be ANYONE BUT JESUS!"

I COULD NOT DISLODGE EVEN ONE SINGLE CARD. NOR COULD I TEAR THE CARDS APART. THEY SEEMED AS STRONG AS STEEL.

I watched, powerless, as the Lord began to open the files and read the cards. I couldn't bear to watch His response. And in the brief moments that I could force myself to look at His face, I saw a sorrow even deeper than my own. He seemed to somehow look inside the very worst boxes. Why did my amazing Lord Jesus have to read every single one?

Finally, He turned and looked at me from across the room. His eyes were like oceans of love and compassion that I could never, ever explain. I dropped my head in shame, covered my face with my hands and began to cry again. I just couldn't bear to look at Him. I had failed Him so miserably. He walked over to me and silently put His arm around me. He didn't say a word. He just cried with me.

"He just cried with me..."

Then, after several minutes, He got up and walked back to the wall of files. Starting at one end of the room, He took out a file and, **one by one, began to sign His name over mine on each card.**

**"IT IS FINISHED."
— JESUS**

I shouted at Him. "No, Jesus! No!" I pulled one of the cards from Him. His name should not be on any of these cards. **But there it was, written in red so rich, so dark, and so alive. The name of Jesus covered mine. It was written with His blood.**

He gently took the card back. He smiled a sad smile and steadily continued the sobering task of signing all the cards with His name and His blood. I don't think I'll ever understand how He did the entire room so quickly. But only an instant later, I heard Him close the final file drawer and walk towards me. His eyes met mine. Once again, I saw love and mercy there that I could never explain nor ever deserve. He spoke three simple words to me:

"It is finished."

Together, we exited the room. There was no lock on the door. Why? I knew instinctively that there were more cards to be written. Yet even more amazing, I knew that His priceless blood and His sacred Name could cancel out my future sin if my trust remained solidly in Him.

Yes, the Bible tells us that one day we will all stand before God to be judged. "So then shall each of us shall give an account of himself to God." (Romans 14:12) All of the "cards" of our life—both good and bad—will be dumped out for the God of the Universe to review. Our only hope on that day will be that because we have put our faith and hope in Jesus Christ, all our sins will be forgiven.

✳✳✳✳✳

Friends, I hope this story impacted you the same way it did me. Every time I hear it, I mourn the number of "cards" I know I have filled with my rotten human choices. But more importantly, I realize that I don't have to (STAY) in the Shadow Room. Like the man in the story, I can walk out knowing that I've been forgiven and that the voices of the Shadow Room don't have to dominate my mind.

But here is the "uncensored truth" for me. *I know that the guilty voices in my head will probably always be there.* Yet there is a voice even louder than the Enemy's. It is the all-faithful and all-loving voice of Jesus. So almost every day of my life, I have to choose once again to let His voice of love and forgiveness drown out the Enemy's haunting lies in my mind. And that, my friend, is an "uncensored choice" I encourage you to make as well.

Note to self:
Re-read this
story often....

\ \ | | ✳ /) / / /

Thank You, Lord, that Your light pierces through all the darkness my sin creates for me. Your voice whispers HOPE to me from "The Shadow Room."

/ / / | | \ \ \ | | \

Thank You that one day in Heaven when I stand before You at the brink of eternity... *Your name, written in Your blood, will be on all my "cards."*

Now that we have talked together about the dark times we all often create for ourselves, let's talk about the dark times God sometimes gives to His kids as divine appointments in our walk with Him. I call these sacred times the *"Darkness of God."* And though I seldom hear anyone talk about this concept, I think these times can become some of God's most amazing love gifts to His kids.

THANK YOU, LORD, THAT YOUR LIGHT PIERCES THROUGH ALL THE DARKNESS MY SIN CREATES FOR ME. YOUR VOICE WHISPERS HOPE TO ME FROM "THE SHADOW ROOM."

So grab another latte...and let's explore a whole different, more positive aspect of those times when God feels far away. This possibility is going to leave you smiling, though.

But first, I need to share some uncensored truth about one of the darkest times in my own life. Sacred truth sometimes comes from sacred darkness. So keep reading...

Thank You that
one day in Heaven
when I stand before
You at the brink
of eternity... Your
name, written in
Your blood, will be
on all my "cards."

When a train goes
through a tunnel
and it gets really
dark, don't panic
and jump off!
Just sit still
and trust the
conductor.

Chapter

06

This is a really important chapter

THE DARKNESS OF GOD

Have you ever been on some of the dark tunnel rides at Disney World? They can be pretty spooky. I mean, all these arms and legs keep reaching out to you from dark corners, freaking you out with unexpected pokes. And the further you go into the tunnel, the darker it gets. You're tempted to say, "Sorry, I made a big mistake getting on this creepy ride. Get me off this thing *before I make a new door in this tunnel!*"

Sometimes, going through the "dark tunnels" with God feels almost the same way. You want to say "let me off this ride." But I'm reminded of a wise old quote that says, *"When a train goes through a tunnel and it gets really dark, don't panic and jump off! Just sit still and trust the Conductor."*

Let me share honestly and openly about one of the darkest "spiritual tunnels" I have ever experienced. I can't tell you how tempted I was to "jump off the ride." It's a time I'll never forget and one I hope I never have to repeat. To be truthful, it's the closest I've ever come to walking away from my Christian faith. I'm not proud to admit it. I had gone through a couple of really rough years, complete with the feeling that God was absolutely nowhere around.

For real— Ever been there?

I tried desperately to "connect" with Him in ways I had experienced before, but nothing seemed to work. The more I tried to "earn" or create some spiritual "feelings" by praying or reading God's Word, the larger the spiritual black hole seemed to become. I call this time period in my life "The Darkness of God." (If I had been given a simple book like this one during that time, it could have saved me a ton of

? ? ? ? ?

confusion and heartache. I guess that's why I wrote this book. I want you to know that you don't have to go through these times alone.)

Then one unforgettable day, I read **Isaiah 50:10** and "the lights came on." (Drum roll, please.) This is another "big deal" verse:

> "Who among you fears the Lord and obeys His servant?
> Let the man who walks in the dark and has no light
> trust in the name of the Lord and rely on his God."

Did you get that? Did you see any fireworks? Probably not. But I wish I could be there with you to light a few. You see, it was like Jesus was giving me specific instructions about what to do while I "walked in darkness and had no light." The words were so simple—yet so revolutionary. Isaiah 50:10 became my lifeline through that "no feeling" season in my walk with Jesus (the first of many to come).

I know what you're thinking. "Glad that verse was such a big deal for you, Jeanne. But it doesn't do much of anything for me."

I understand. But let me walk you through the verse like the Lord did with me that day. I think it will come to have a deep meaning and hope for you, too. (Please run around the room and do push-ups if you need to wake up and get the blood pumping. These next few paragraphs may save your spiritual life one day.)

01. *"Who among you fears the Lord and obeys His servant?"* The Lord used these words to clearly show me that God is talking to His own spiritual kids in this verse. So the person who *"walks in the dark and has no light"* has to be a Christian, not a nonbeliever. What's the obvious conclusion? Good Christians sometimes walk through seasons where it feels pretty dark and dry. There's no indication here that the person did anything wrong to bring the darkness on himself.

GOD'S CHARACTER CAN BE TRUSTED WHEN YOUR FEELINGS CAN'T.

Wow! That was a big deal to me. You see, I had been beating myself up big time, thinking that some hidden sin had caused me to lose feeling and made me spiritually numb. I now realize that even committed Christians sometimes feel far from God— through no fault of their own.

02. *"Who walks in the dark..."* What are you supposed to do when the "spiritual black-out" comes? Keep

walking! Spiritually, don't let yourself "sit down on the inside"—no matter how tempting it might be to quit. Keep on doing what the Lord told you to do "before the lights went out." Keep praying...keep reading the Word...keep believing ... keep loving...just keep doing what you know to do. It's really important now because you can't let your feelings be your guide. If you let yourself "sit down" on the inside, "spiritual rigor mortis" can start to set in. Spiritual slumps are a lot like a comfortable bed—easy to fall into, but tough *True* to crawl out of. ☹

03. *"Trust in the name of the Lord..."* **In Old Testament times, a person's name was a big deal.** People were given names that depicted their character. So when it says here "trust in the *name* of the Lord," it's telling us to trust big time in His CHARACTER. Please remember: *God's character can be trusted when your feelings can't.* So no matter how you feel or how rough the circumstances look, you can trust that everything is going to be OK because the Lord's character never

Always, Always, Always

changes. He is always faithful...always just...always loving...always wise...always your Father... AND ALWAYS EVERYTHING YOU NEED HIM TO BE. When Jesus is all you have, Jesus is all you need.

04. *"And rely on his God."* In the Hebrew language the word translated *rely* means, "to lean heavily upon." So when you're going through dark, tough times, the Lord is telling you to "lean heavily" on Him and His Word. Have you ever leaned back on someone and put all your weight against them? I do it once in awhile to my husband. And I know one simple thing: If he moves even a few inches, I'm in trouble! I'll lose my balance and fall because I'm putting all my trust in him to hold me up.

Lean on me! When you're not strong...

It's the same thing when you're walking through the dark times spiritually. Just "lean hard" on the Lord, His character and His Word. He promises He won't ever move—not even a few inches. And while you're "leaning," let me give you something else to smile

about. God's promises are like stars. The darker the
night, the brighter they shine. ☆ *Wow! Really good* ←

HOW LONG WILL THE "DARKNESS" LAST?

I can't begin to tell you when some of the "feelings"
will return in your relationship
with Christ. Sometimes the dark,
spiritually numb times last for only a
couple of days. Other times, they last
much longer. But on the other side
of the "black hole," I promise that
your spiritual roots will be deeper
and your faith will be stronger. Even
more important, you'll make Jesus

WHEN JESUS IS ALL YOU HAVE, JESUS IS ALL YOU NEED.

smile because of the authentic friendship you're developing
with Him. You see, He's got a lot of "casual friends" who
just stick around when times are good and emotions are
high. Try not to be a "friend" like that. Jesus deserves **real**

Not good ☹

THE DARKNESS OF GOD

friendship from you, not just the superficial, self-serving kind.

Thinking about being stuck in the dark reminds me of one of my favorite stories. A 5-year-old boy named Josh got separated from his mom in the middle of a large, busy grocery store. To make matters worse, it was near the store's closing time. Soon, the big overhead lights automatically turned off, and Josh was stranded in the dim shadows of long, towering grocery shelves.

Josh

The child panicked as he ran from one darkened aisle to another, desperately hunting for his mom. Finally, in sheer exhaustion, he collapsed hopelessly on the floor and began to cry. His search seemed agonizingly impossible. His young, scared heart wondered if he would he ever find his mom again.

Within moments, though, Josh's devoted mom followed the sound of his crying and found his shaking little body huddled on the floor. She wrapped her arms tightly around him and said softly, "Josh, if it ever gets really dark, and you feel separated from momma again, here's all you have to do. Don't start running around in fear. *INSTEAD, JUST STAY STILL RIGHT WHERE YOU ARE AND KEEP CALLING MY NAME.*"

Goose bump moment

That's great advice for us as God's kids, don't you think? We all experience spiritually dark times—times when we feel lost or separated from our loving Heavenly Father—and we're tempted to let confusion and fear take over. But running in circles will get us nowhere. What's our answer?

Don't panic in the darkness. Just **"stay steady right where you are and keep calling His name."**

Loneliness is
God's cry for
friendship time

with me.

Chapter

07

SOLITARY CONFINEMENT

The dark, unfeeling times in our walk with God have a close "second cousin" called loneliness. Which comes first, the loneliness or the dark times? I'm not really sure. All I know is that they often walk together. So let me relive a recent personal experience with a friend who faced her own episode of "solitary confinement." I think you'll relate.

The door to the office was barely cracked open. As I walked past, I heard the muffled sound of someone I cared about—crying. I froze in my steps, not knowing if I should step into the office or pretend I had heard nothing. My gut instinct told me to go on in. So I tapped lightly on the door and slipped inside. Her eyes met mine. They revealed a strange mixture of hurt, fear and anger.

I paused for a moment, searching for words. Then I softly said, "Can I do anything to help?"

I can relate to that!

"My life is really screwed up," she muttered. Then her head pointed back down towards the floor. She paused to gain her composure and kept talking.

"I feel so alone, Jeanne," she said. "And to make matters worse, God doesn't seem to be around either. I can't tell you the last time I prayed and felt like somebody was actually listening to me. I don't have any decent friends and even God seems to have taken a hike. It's like living your whole life in solitary confinement."

Blah... Blah... Blah...

I didn't want to be the dispenser of T.R.T. ("Typical Religious Talk"). But I took a risk and asked another question.

"Do you think there might be a link between your loneliness and the feeling that God is a million miles away?" I softly asked her. "You know, the solitary confinement feeling."

She lifted her head and a glimmer of hope flashed quickly through her eyes. "Maybe," she said. "Maybe...but even if the two do connect, where do I go from here? The hole in my heart is growing bigger each day. It's like both God and my friends have taken a long, distant vacation."

"My friend," I answered knowingly. "Let me take you for a cup of coffee. I want to share some things I've learned about loneliness. I think it might even help with the feelings that God's moved out of town."

"Out of town?" she laughed nervously as we stood to leave. "You can say that again. And He didn't even leave a forwarding address."

Have you ever been so lonely that you felt like both God and your friends "moved away"—and left no forwarding address? I sure have.

Counselors call loneliness "the emotional epidemic of the decade." We all have our cell phones, Blackberries,

Facebook pages and laptops. We really are living in the "communication age." Yet in the middle of it all, we've become increasingly technology-rich but friendship-poor.

God knows that this loneliness deal has always been a big problem for His people. By the time we hit only the second chapter of the Bible, He starts talking about it. Read Genesis 2:18 for yourself. He said, "It isn't good for man to be ALONE." So let me walk you through some of the things I shared with my friend over coffee that day. Maybe it will help you like it's helped me—and her.

You see, true loneliness is not so much an absence of AFFECTION or ATTENTION...but an absence of DIRECTION. When lonely feelings start to crowd in on me, I use them as a loving signal from my Heavenly Dad that **He misses me.**

 That's why I often remind myself that **"loneliness becomes my *friend* when it forces me to draw companionship from God that I would normally try to draw from other people."** It's not an easy answer, but it's one that works. I promise. Remember, we called this book *Uncensored.*

I'VE LEARNED TO TURN LONELINESS INTO ALONENESS.

(Get that? Sounds profound, but it really has saved my "spiritual neck" a bunch of times.) Now don't wimp out and stop reading. In the next chapter, I'll tell you how to turn loneliness into aloneness. But first, let me show you the difference between the two:

LONELINESS	VS.	ALONENESS
Basically stinks! *Sure does* →	→	Can be your ticket to a more fulfilling, meaningful life.
Takes no willful choice of my own.	→	Takes a conscious CHOICE on my part. (In other words, I stop whining and CHOOSE!)
Has no obvious purpose.	→	Allows me time to explore and deepen my own personal sense of destiny and purpose.
Focuses on "me" and is self-centered.	→	Focuses beyond "me" and usually becomes other-centered.
Takes up residence in "Depression City, U.S.A."	→	Brings real joy and peace (not the phony kind that goes up and down with circumstances).

LONELINESS	VS.	ALONENESS
Is a turn-off to the opposite sex.	⟶	Produces inward security that makes you increasingly MORE ATTRACTIVE to the opposite sex. (I've got you interested now, don't I?) Sure do!
Creates isolation, doubt, and pain.	⟶	Creates intimacy with the Lord, because you really can grow gradually to recognize Him as your Best Friend.
Is used by the enemy for his purpose.	⟶	Is used by the heavenly Father for HIS PURPOSES.

If someone asked me to pin-point one of the most life-changing prayers I've ever prayed, it would be an easy answer: "Lord, I don't want to be stuck in the ruts of my own loneliness. Give me the guts to make the right choices—to turn *loneliness* into *aloneness.*" I can't tell you what a big deal this simple concept has been for me. It's made *all the difference* in my human relationships as well as when God feels a million miles away.

RIGHT CHOICES EVENTUALLY BRING RIGHT EMOTIONS.

Keep reading, and I'll help you put this principle to work in your own life. I have to warn you though. YOU are going to have to decide to make the right choices, even when you don't feel like it. I can't decide for you. I do have some good news though. Right choices eventually bring right emotions.

P.S. Did I mention you're supposed to do this stuff even when you don't feel like it?

Loneliness becomes your friend when it forces you to draw companionship from God that you would normally try to draw from other people.

LONELINESS...
A GOOD THING?

Have you ever stopped to consider how loneliness can be a good thing? For real. It all pivots around *what we do with the loneliness when it comes crashing in around us.* I know one thing for sure: PEOPLE DON'T REMOVE LONELINESS. I started experiencing the truth of those words in college. Let me share my story.

I clearly remember the fall evening at school when my whole perspective on loneliness changed. I had just broken up with a guy I cared for very much. For several different reasons though, I knew the guy was not for me. So obeying the Lord felt good, but the loneliness stunk. Late that night, I was complaining to the Lord about how isolated I felt. The women's dorm was almost empty. Everyone was out for some Saturday night fun with friends. The silence on my hall echoed loudly into my heart. Then, five simple words cut through the silence, like a megaphone in my head: *"Turn the loneliness into aloneness."*

Now I've got to tell you. I'm not one who gets a million "words from God." But somehow, this time seemed special and different. I had never heard the phrase "turn the loneliness into aloneness" before. Yet that night, it seemed to resonate with hope and purpose. Many years have now passed since that lonely Saturday night as a junior in college, but those five words have become an anchor for my voyage with Christ. I guess it all pivots around the quote, *"Loneliness becomes my FRIEND when it forces me to draw companionship from God that I would normally try to draw from OTHER PEOPLE."*

So how do you make this mystical, life-changing exchange? How do you turn loneliness into aloneness?

Let me share four simple principles that have guided my journey through the years. By the way, if you're starting to fall asleep right now—WAKE UP! This is another really important part. (I hear you laughing because I've said that before, but this really is life-changing. Besides, you wouldn't be reading it if you didn't want to know.)

NO ONE ELSE IN THE UNIVERSE TAKES YOUR PLACE IN GOD'S HEART.

Just grab some coffee, plug your brain in all the way and let's talk about the four things you can do to turn loneliness into aloneness:

Step #1 = Recognize feelings of loneliness as God's cry for friendship time with you.   #1

Ever heard that before? I sure hope so because I put it in bold print in the last chapter! It will be a life-changing revelation when you realize that <u>our heavenly Father gets LONELY for you at times.</u>   Really?

Tomorrow morning, I will hop in my car and drive back to Atlanta. (I've been hiding out for a few days, attempting to get quite a bit of "UNCENSORED" knocked out.) But let me tell you some good news. My incredible husband is LONELY for me! He's had a thousand other people around him while I've been gone. But I guarantee that no one else has taken my place in his heart.

Mind-blowing as it is, no one else in the whole universe takes your place in God's heart. So realize that it's one of the highest honors in the world to be told that "God is lonely for friendship time with you." The day I began to recognize loneliness as God's desire to "hang out with me," MY WHOLE PERCEPTION CHANGED. Suddenly, loneliness signaled an unbelievable invitation from the God of the Universe to spend time together. Look at it this way: Someone far more important than the President of the United States is hoping to hang out with you soon. Wow—that's pretty mind-blowing!

> **Step #2 = Talk back to your emotions rather than letting your emotions do all the talking.** #2

Sounds a little psycho, but David gives us a great example of this in Psalm 42. I guess it proves that great people really *do* talk to themselves. David says, "Why are you discouraged, my soul? Why are you restless deep inside yourself?... Instead, choose to put your hope and trust in God."

Way to go, Dave!

Forgive the old language, but let me tell you what *the soul* refers to when you read it in the Old Testament. It refers to a person's **"mind, will, and emotions."** So what David was really saying here is: "Why are you discouraged, David, *in your own mind?* Why are you letting discouragement win out *in your will?* And why are you letting those lonely, discouraged *feelings have such control of your emotions?*"

Self... Knock it off!

David gives us a great pattern for healthy, Christ-honoring "talking back to ourselves." Counselors call this whole concept "controlling our self-talk." It's a big, big deal. Feelings don't come just from circumstances. Feelings are created after circumstances are filtered through our mind, will, and emotions. I'm not suggesting that if a truck runs over your head that you should pretend to be happy about it. I just want us all to realize that negative junk happens in everyone's life. You and you alone determine the mental and emotional "filter" through which you see all those events. Simply put, your life will be much happier if you learn to control your mind, will, and emotions rather than letting your emotions to constantly control you.

In your present life, who is doing the most "talking"— your emotions or your will?

#3 (Step #3 = Choose.)

That's not too profound, is it? Millions of people think about making certain choices without ever making a real change in their daily lifestyles. They may have great intentions, but they never seem to take action.

Take a few nights ago, for example. I was lonely. I had spoken to a crowd of several thousand people. The night

Pity Pity Pity
Pity Pity Pity Pity

had gone great, but around midnight, I found myself back in my empty hotel room, staring at the walls. Self-pity started to creep its way into my emotions. (I laughingly say that sometimes I like to feel sorry for myself because I can do it so much better than anyone else I know! I don't just throw "pity parties" for myself; sometimes I throw "pity banquets"!)

I had a simple choice that night in the hotel. I could either let the loneliness become more gripping, or I could choose to apply the principles I'm writing about. (Granted, it's a lot easier to *write* about these principles than it is to *live them*.) So I crawled out of bed, put on one of my favorite worship CD's, picked up my journal and started to write. The opening lines in that night's journal entry went something like this...

> YOUR LIFE WILL BE MUCH HAPPIER IF YOU LEARN TO CONTROL YOUR MIND, WILL, AND EMOTIONS—RATHER THAN LETTING YOUR EMOTIONS CONSTANTLY CONTROL YOU.

"OK, Jesus. I'm writing in my next book about turning loneliness into aloneness. So I guess, one more time, I'm going to choose to do it myself. It's

strange how making the right decision feels so dramatically "undramatic" the moment I make it. But somehow, right choices eventually bring right emotions. So here we go again, Lord. Help me to direct my aching need for a friend tonight towards You. Who knows? Maybe You're feeling pretty lonely right now, too."

So what made me a hero that night? One simple, non-profound thing: *I chose.* Years ago, I had a sign in my office that read, *"When you don't FEEL like praying, TALK TO GOD about it!"* That's the choice I've made over and over again. And I encourage you to do the same thing: CHOOSE.

#4   Step #4 = Reach out to others and *give away* the very emotions you yourself would like to receive.

The Bible says bluntly, "Whatever you give away to others will be given back to you." It's a principle that works in every arena of life. So when I'm lonely, I know one quick way out is to reach beyond myself. Now this can be a little tricky. You see, loneliness is really SELF-centered. "**S.E.L.F.**" stands for "**S**atan's **E**xact **L**ocation **F**orever." So, if I let myself respond in the natural, human way, I won't want to reach (beyond myself) (As a matter of fact, the lonelier I am, the more I want to crawl into bed and pull the covers up over my head!)

But if you push past that self-centeredness, amazing things await on the other side. If you need someone to listen to you, search for someone you can listen to. If you

> **WHEN YOU DON'T FEEL LIKE PRAYING, TALK TO GOD ABOUT IT!**

need someone to encourage you, hunt for someone you can encourage first. I don't know how it works. I just know that it's a scriptural law that never, ever fails. It's called "the law of sowing and reaping." Unselfishly give away what you want yourself...and somehow, some way it will always come back to you...multiplied.

Sound tough? Well, think of Jesus. While He was hanging on the cross, He was experiencing the most painful, lonely time of His entire life. Yet in the middle of that gut-wrenching loneliness, He chose to reach out to those around Him. He gave encouragement and life to the thief dying on the cross next to Him. Then He looked down from the cross and made sure His mother, Mary, was taken care of. In a final act of incredible unselfishness, Christ prayed that His Father would forgive the very people who were taking His life. In short, Jesus gave us a mind-blowing example of someone who kept giving to others emotionally at a time when He most needed emotional support Himself.

The result? Well, the Bible makes it pretty clear that on Resurrection Day, Jesus was one "Happy Camper." And unless my theology is confused, I don't think He's experienced many "dark, depressing days" since that time. Now don't get me wrong. I'm not suggesting that you go hunt for a cross to die on. I am suggesting, though, that you shake yourself out of a self-centered focus and purposefully choose to give away the very emotions you would really like to receive yourself.

How does it work? Beats me. All I know is that it works— every single time. It may not be in that exact same hour or day. But somehow, Jesus fills your heart with the very emotions you chose to give away to someone else.

Remember: **God will be no man's debtor.** What's that saying? Just that you can <u>never</u>, <u>ever</u> out-give God. Whatever you give away in His name, He will always multiply back to you. **And that even includes gifts of the heart**

Personal note from Jeanne: Remember the story at the opening of this chapter about the night in college when I broke up with a guy and loneliness began to overwhelm me? A couple weeks later, in my attempts to turn the loneliness into aloneness, I journaled these thoughts in the form of a prayer. Let me share them with you. Though many years have passed since the time of its writing, I still connect deeply to the words I wrote that night.

SOMETIMES GOD IS LONELY TOO

From My Heart to You, Lord:

The empty, lonely feeling is back again, Jesus.

You know, the one that always comes when my need for a "someone"

takes over.

I sit waiting for the phone to ring...

Contriving all sorts of schemes in my fantasies...

Re-playing old moments together like treasured home movies in my

    mind.

But still the loneliness remains...

Still the need for closeness screams out in my empty world.

You know the longing, Father...for You gave it to me.

It's the longing to give myself to someone completely...totally...

    exclusively.

To have a friend who cuts through the darkness and everyday chatter

And dares to make a place within the living room of my heart.

Is it fair to ask, at least, that the aching emptiness be lifted

If, for this time, I walk alone?

 ## From the Father's Heart Back to Me:

Loneliness, Jeanne? I know it all too well.

For while you contrive your endless schemes for friendship,

I am often left alone...My heart left to ache with yearnings for <u>YOUR</u>
<u>friendship</u>.

When will you ever learn?
It will not be until you are satisfied with being loved by Me alone
That you will be capable of such a human relationship.

And even then, the emptiness will, in part, remain.
For the deepest part of your heart will remain restless
Until it rests in Me.
Every other relationship will be elusive,
Captivated by peaks and valleys.
I, and I alone, can speak peace to the lonely aching of your heart.

Can you not trust Me?
Just as surely as I have given you the desire for companionship,
I will fulfill it.
<u>I want you to see in flesh a tangible picture of My deep love and</u>
<u>commitment to you</u>.

Yet, do not impatiently hurry away.

What you cry FOR today...

You may well cry ABOUT tomorrow.

Can I just be enough for you?

Can we laugh together...cry together ...

And be friends like we once were?

For while you scream out for another human being,

My Father-heart screams out for you.

So run away restlessly again, Jeanne...to barter for your needs.

But I will wait here patiently for you.

For I too am empty...

I too am yearning...

I too am lonely...

Lonely, my child, for you.

"What you cry FOR today, you may well cry ABOUT tomorrow."
—Jesus

"Destiny is not a matter of choice; it is a matter of choice. It is not to be waited for; it is a thing to be achieved."

Hmmm... I wonder if it actually works??

eHARMONY'S ADVICE ON DEALING WITH THE DARK TIMES

OK, stop laughing. Maybe you're not a big eHarmony fan. Truth be told, neither am I. But Dr. Neil Clark Warren, founder of eHarmony, is onto something. He's helped hundreds of thousands of people deal with the lonely, dark times we're talking about. (He's got his own system of turning "loneliness into aloneness!") He provides online personality tests and matches as *his* solution to the empty, relationally dark times we all sometimes experience.

Dr. Neil

Many of these couples even vow that Dr. Warren has helped them create a "match made in heaven." I'm sure

Woo Hoo... Sign me up!!

you've seen the commercials. He's been on thousands of radio and television programs. Even Oprah gives him her stamp or approval! So what's the guy got to say about combating the "dark times" and creating relational happiness? I took the time to find out so I could pass it on to you. (Aren't I a great friend? Now you don't have to pay money to find out his "bottom lines.") After all, his years of experience should give him some pretty decent relational clues.

Oprah

Stamp of Approval!

So here it is. Dr. Warren says that if you want to be truly happy and "live the good life," it will boil down to *three simple things.* He calls them the "Hallmarks of Health." He says loneliness in our lives is combated by purposefully cultivating three simple, but important ingredients in our day-to-day living. Let's take a run at it:

01.   *Profound significance*—In other words, happy people know someone loves them unconditionally, to the very core of their being. In my world, that "someone" is **Jesus Christ.** Sure, I've got the greatest husband and family in the universe. But long before they ever entered my life, I had the "profound significance"

AKA: No matter what!

thing going for me. You see, no matter how great my human relationships might be, they can never consistently meet all my deep longings on the inside— all my needs for "someone."

Read this again

I don't think that any human relationship can deliver that kind of unfaltering mind-reading and need-meeting. That's why I've chosen to build my sense of "profound significance" around my relationship with Christ. His Word guarantees me that even during the "dark, unfeeling times," He's still right by my side—believing in me and cheering me on.

HAPPY PEOPLE KNOW SOMEONE LOVES THEM UNCONDITIONALLY.

Beyond that, my life has a **purpose and meaning** in Christ that pulls me through the dark times and gives me a reason to get out of bed in the morning. You're part of that purpose right now! I've got a publishing deadline to meet that dragged me out of my warm bed this morning (even though the covers whispered, "Stay here with us, Jeanne!"). Now don't get nervous

Stay here with us, Jeanne!

about this "purpose and meaning" thing. You don't need to be Billy Graham, Bill Gates, or Barack Obama to develop a sense of deep significance for your life.

 Significance does not come from being famous but from having purpose. You need to decide for yourself who and what you are living for. Do you know?

02. *Unswerving authenticity*—Wow, what's that mean?
Our eHarmony friend defines it as people who know who they really are. They're people who are courageously committed to living out their true personality and God-given talents. Granted, it's super easy during the dark times to lose the core of who you really are. It's even easier during the lonely times to frantically begin to blend in with others just so you feel some friendship. But "eHarmony man" says that's a big mistake if you want true fulfillment. He tells you to remain authentic to the person God has wired YOU to be! Don't remake yourself for someone else's acceptance. Didn't some famous guy years ago say, "To your own self be true"? Better yet, I'm reminded

of a little kid's poster that reads, "**You were born an original. Don't die a copy.**" Need I say more?

03. *Self-sacrificing love—***You knew that was coming, didn't you?** You can't be truly happy and relationally fulfilled unless you give yourself away to other people. (And let me be clear. I'm not talking sexually.) But sometimes, when you're in the middle of the heavy darkness and loneliness, that's a pretty big challenge. Instead of wanting to give yourself away, you instinctively want to curl up in a ball and pull the covers up over your head. Relate?

That's in the first "Uncensored" book!

But the eHarmony guy says this approach will only spell more darkness for us. He says that happy people focus on giving themselves away. It's the Biblical principle of giving away to others what we most long for ourselves. So give yourself away to a cause or meaning bigger than your own selfish desires. It will change everything. And it doesn't have to be giving away a million dollars. You can give yourself away in the little moments. So when you need someone to

Good...
Cause I spent all my $ on this book!

listen to you, purposefully choose to listen to someone else. When you wish someone would deliver a Starbucks surprise to your desk, do it for someone else instead. And the results are pretty fantastic. Seneca had it all figured out back in 4 B.C. when he said, *"If you want to be loved, love."*

So congratulations! You don't have to be a shrink to figure things out during the dark, lonely seasons of life. But I think we can all agree that the eHarmony guy is onto something. True happiness can be boiled down to *getting right with* [God] (significance), *getting right with* [yourself] (authenticity) and *getting right with* [others] (love). However, none of that has anything to do with having a significant other; you can actually achieve each of Dr. Warren's "Hallmarks of Health" while you are still single.

Easy? Not exactly. Profound? You bet. But the choice is up to you. Maybe that's why William Jennings Bryan said, "Destiny is not a matter of chance; it is a matter of choice. It is not a thing to be waited for; it is a thing to be achieved."

(Footnote: Adapted from *Love the Life You Live* by Neil Clark Warren and Les Parrott [Tyndale House Publishers, Wheaton, Illinois, 2004, page 11].)

True happiness can be boiled down to getting right with God (significance), getting right with yourself (authenticity) and getting right with others (love).

Single
1: Ugly ≠
2: Lonely
3: Incomplete

"Single" means:
1: "To be SEPARATE"

2: "To be UNIQUE"

3: "To be WHOLE"

Chapter

10

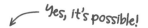 *Yes, it's possible!*

SUCCESSFULLY SINGLE—
AND SATISFIED

I married the greatest man in the world. His name is
Sam (I may have mentioned him once or twice before), and
he's honestly my greatest earthly hero. Sometimes when
I talk about him in public, I sing part of Bette Midler's
legendary song, "Wind Beneath My Wings," to describe
him.

> "... *Did you ever know that you're my hero?*
> *You're everything I wish I could be.*
> *I can fly higher than an eagle.*
> *'Cause you are the wind beneath my wings."*

He's my hero for countless reasons. But let me focus on just one for a minute: **He taught me the beauty of singleness.** Now, let me pause here. You might be confused. You might even be thinking, "Hold up, Jeanne, just a moment ago, we were talking about finding God in the dark times, and now you're talking about your husband and how he taught you about the beauty of singleness?!" Well, let's be honest. For many people, being single is one of the biggest dark times in life. So I want to take a minute (or

Sad but true ⟶

maybe even two or three) to talk about this whole "single" thing from a different perspective. Maybe you're like me; I thought being single was a serious bummer. And then I met Sam. He really gave me a different way to look at things.

One night over pizza—while Sam and I were still single—I asked him what some of his goals were. He shared with me some awesome dreams. But one of his goals was particularly attractive to me. He said, "Jeanne, until it's time for me to tie the knot, **I want to be successfully single.**" I had never heard anyone say that before. He really had my attention.

Sam shared with me that God's idea of singleness is not the empty, lonely season in life that many of us make it. In Genesis 2:18, God did (NOT) say, "It is not good for man to be SINGLE." He said, "It is not good that man should be ALONE." Singleness (when lived God's way) is a positive, fulfilling season in life.

To drive home his point a little more, Sam pulled out the dictionary and looked up the word, "single." Here are three definitions he highlighted:

"Single" means: #1: "To be SEPARATE"

#2: "To be UNIQUE"

#3: "To be WHOLE"

If that's the true definition of singleness ("to be separate, unique, and whole"), **then being truly single should be one of our top goals in life!** That's why instead of running away from being single, we should be running toward singleness. Instead of blaming singleness for many of our dark times, singleness can become our friend. It allows us time to figure out who we really are—to develop our own identity in Christ. If you don't know who YOU are yet, don't kid yourself into believing that you'll really "find yourself" inside a serious relationship. Believe me, the picture only gets messier!

Sam had somehow grabbed ahold of the difference between being "single" and being "alone." Because he seemed to understand some of the benefits of a season of singleness, he "milked" this period in his life for all it was worth—determined to make something positive of it. Sure, he wanted to be married one day. But he chose to be (secure) instead of (needy.) And because of that security, he didn't fall prey to the desire to date and marry for the wrong reasons.

IF MARRIAGE IS THE KEY TO HAPPINESS, THEN JESUS WOULD HAVE BEEN ONE DEPRESSED GUY.

Our "pizza discussion" continued. "I've tried to really cash in on these years," he said to me. **"After all, a SUCCESSFUL MARRIAGE is only the product of two people who were first SUCCESSFULLY SINGLE."**

Bam!!!

$1+1=2$

We had a fun talk that night, both of us venting our frustration over friends who thought the key to all earthly bliss was matrimony. We even got a little profound as the evening progressed. **"After all,"** we agreed, **"if marriage is the key to happiness, then Jesus would have been one depressed guy."**

Never thought about that...

Whether or not you agree with our theology of that statement, Sam's view on singleness made him very, very attractive to me. (Did I say "VERY attractive!"?) You see, truly "single" people ("unique and whole") are the most fascinating people in the universe. They have <u>vision</u>, <u>goals</u>, and <u>plans</u> for their lives that make them <u>incredibly</u> <u>complete</u> and <u>radically interesting</u>. Many of the other guys I dated were everything but "unique and whole." Their biggest mission in life seemed to be to find a mate. To me, that seemed like a pretty shallow ambition.

Sam was different. He saw singleness as a vital, important season of life. "After all," he said that night, "it's something God gave you FIRST before anything else." Other guys I dated during college had a really different approach to their singleness—and their attempts to "win" me. They would say stuff like...

- "I can't live without you, Jeanne."

- "I'll never be all I could be without you in my life."

- Then there was the "ace card" of all Christian relationships—"I've prayed, Jeanne, and I think you're the will of God for my life!" (That got nerve-wracking, because seven different guys in college told me that. I guess God kept changing His mind!)

7 guys vs. God

To me, all those come-ons didn't seem at all romantic. They just made the guys come across as needy, weak and addictive. You see, some people get addicted to drugs. But other people get addicted to a person (or their NEED for another person). I just wasn't excited about signing up for that kind of life. My thinking was that life is too short to spend it baby-sitting someone else. I wanted to enter a relationship one day where we were "husband and wife" — not the other person's "mommy or daddy."

Here's a big thought. Are you ready? **Your marriage will only be as successful as your singleness. You can only bring into a marriage who and what you are as a single person. Healthy marriages aren't "50-50." They're "100-100."** Each person must give himself or herself completely and exclusively to the other.

So what's my suggestion? Stop whining about being single. I know that realistically, the lonely, dark times will come, but capture this season with all the passion and purpose you can bring to the table. **Don't spend so much time looking for *who you want* that you have no time to be *who you are.*** Use every waking moment to develop yourself into being ***SUCCESSFULLY*** SINGLE—"more unique" and "more whole." And if you ever need more motivation for this approach, just watch many of the married couples around you. You'll probably find that their faces don't exactly shout, "Happily ever after!"

Shine— Don't whine!

What did I just hear some of you say? You're not sure if you like my perspective of working towards being "Successfully Single"? Hey, it's a free country. Develop your own philosophy. All I can tell you is that MINE WORKED. My boyfriend and I have been happily married for nearly 40 years now. Be sure to check back with me after your approach has been successful for a few decades. I look forward to hearing from you. In the mean time, my husband and I are going out tonight for a date.

www.ProveMeWrongIn40yrs.org

P.S. Did I say, "Quit whining!" yet? People are so incredibly unattractive when they come across as lonely and pitiful. Sorry for the bluntness. But if you want your "ever after" to be happy, please grab on to this uncensored truth. And let me add another honest reflection. No matter how amazing your marriage may be, you'll still experience some "dark times" when it feels like God is a million miles away. Sorry for the reality check. But no human being can ever shelter you from the dark times of spiritual life. Not even your spouse.

If you liked this chapter, you should read the 1st Uncensored book on relationships and SEX!

RAW TALK ON DATING, FRIENDSHIP, AND SEX

An exciting text message? A great friendship gone south? A riveting stop on the Internet? A lonely night at home? Step into the world of a million different opportunities—the world of relationships.

Jeanne Mayo, renowned youth culture expert, talks bluntly about topics that most don't have the guts to address at all. Inside *UNCENSORED* you will find hard hitting feedback on dating, friendship, falling in love, masturbation, determining your future, sex, homosexual struggles, and more. Avoid the pitfalls. It's your life. It's your choice. It's worth getting the facts.

Order books @ www.youthleaderscoach.com

Sometimes when
I'm feeling God
the least, I
may actually
be pleasing
God the most.

THE DAY JESUS COULDN'T FEEL GOD'S PRESENCE EITHER

It was the darkest day in all of history. Jesus, with blood gushing from every inch of His body, hung in agony on the cross. Then came the thunder, sending chills down each onlooker's spine. Suddenly, Jesus shouts to the heavens six unforgettable words:

> *"Father, why have You abandoned Me?"*

Come on, God. This isn't fair. Here's Your Son dying for the whole world, and He can't even feel Your presence? How does that work?

I know Bible teachers would give us lots of possible answers. But maybe—just maybe—God was trying to help us out here. Maybe He knew that one of our most difficult "crosses" in life would be when we hit those "no feeling times" in our walk with Him. You know, the times when you want to look up to Heaven and say, "Father, why have You abandoned me?"

So let me remind you of something incredibly awesome. Jesus Christ did His most hell-defying, God-honoring work when He felt absolutely DESERTED by God the Father. No angels showed up at the cross to sing worship songs to Him. Nearly all of His closest friends had ditched Him. One of His tightest disciples even cussed in fear, denying he even knew Jesus. God didn't dispatch any "angelic special agents" to whisper words of encouragement to His Son that day. Yet in the middle of feeling about as "unspiritual" as one could get, Jesus changed the course of all history!

Does that give you hope? It sure does me. It reminds me that sometimes when I'm feeling God the LEAST, I may actually be pleasing God the MOST.

Let me wrap up our time together with a (true story) from the time of the Jewish Holocaust and Nazi imprisonments. It really <u>echoes</u> what I've been trying to share with you about finding God when He feels far away.

> JESUS CHRIST DID HIS MOST HELL-DEFYING, GOD-HONORING WORK WHEN HE FELT ABSOLUTELY DESERTED BY GOD THE FATHER.

When the Nazi's were defeated around 1945, the Allies raced victoriously into the prison camps to release the remaining captives. Though most of the captives during the Holocaust were Jews, many Christian ministers had also been imprisoned by the Germans. The prison camp at Dachau held an especially large group of Christian ministers.

Amid the excitement, two American soldiers broke into a dark cell at Dachau to release three pastors who had been confined there for years. The soldiers weren't prepared for what they saw. Two frail ministers wept softly in one corner of the cell. The third minister—their comrade and friend—had taken his last breath only moments before freedom arrived.

The Allied soldiers respectfully asked to help carry the minister's body out of the dirty cell for a proper burial. As they did, they noticed that the minister's right index finger was nothing more than a bloody stub.

"Was this part of how they tortured him?" the Allied soldier asked one of the other ministers. He assumed that the pastor's finger had been amputated as part of the Nazis' cruel punishment.

"No, that's not how it happened," the minister answered. The cell grew quiet as he fought to regain his composure. Then he pointed towards the crumbling brick wall at the end of the darkness. "Go read what it says," he told the Allied soldier. "That's how his finger became so short. He used it as his pen."

"A pen?" the soldier asked, still not grasping what had happened.

"Yeah... He spent hours every day re-tracing the message he left on that wall. He pressed so hard that his blood became the ink. As the months passed, his finger became shorter and shorter from the pressure. That's how it became so small. But our friend was determined that the Nazi's would not defeat his faith. He wanted to leave a message for the whole world to read."

The dark cell filled with a sacred reverence. The Allied soldiers gently placed the minister's dead body on the old cot again. Then, without a word, they walked closer to the dark, crumbling bricks where the message had been painstakingly scrawled. On the walls of that Nazi prison cell, the man had written:

"I believe in the sun...even when it is not shining.

I believe in love...even when I cannot feel it.

And I believe in God...even when He is silent."

What powerful words: "I believe in God...even when He is silent." How life-changing. How costly.

And so, my friend, here's my final question to you: What "message" are you writing on the "walls of your life"? In a world of shallow Christianity that changes with every passing emotion, may your commitment to Christ be grounded in **His** Word—not *your* feelings. That one decision will make you a Christ-follower of rare, "uncensored" character.

And so, may it be said of us one day, "They believed in God—even when He was silent."

Live courageously, my friend—even in the darkness.

Live courageously!

Lovingly,
Jeanne

Live
courageously,
my friend—

Even in the
darkness.

Live courageously!

THE INVITATION OF A LIFETIME

Do you remember how you felt on Christmas morning when you were a little kid? The excitement was just too much to handle! I remember getting up early, sneaking downstairs to look at all my wrapped gifts and then bombarding my parents' bed so they would "get up and start to open the presents!"

Most of those gifts were short-lived. I mean, the bikes eventually rusted and the other toys quickly fell apart. Truth be told, I eventually just lost interest in most of them.

There's really only one gift I've ever received that has weathered the ultimate test of time. An earlier book, *Uncensored: Dating, Friendship, and Sex*, is an honest book about relationships, and let me tell you the most important thing I have ever discovered: There is only one relationship in the universe that has never disappointed me, never been too busy too deeply connect with me and never left me with some aching emptiness on the inside.

For real...

That gift would be my personal relationship with Jesus Christ.

114

We make this whole thing about knowing Christ way too tough. It's not about what "religion" we are (or aren't), what clothes we wear or how many great things in life we manage to pull off. Real relationship with Christ begins when we choose to sincerely ask Christ into our life to be our Best Friend, our Savior and our Lord.

It's the "lordship" part that throws a lot of people off. You see, Jesus is kind of like my husband on this count. Sam Mayo doesn't want to be "*one* of Jeanne's husbands." He wants to be "*the* man" in my life. And wisely, Jesus Christ gave his life on the cross for you so He could earn the right to be "*the Man*" in your life. He doesn't want "a piece of the pie." He wants the whole thing. He never asks for perfection. He knows we'll all mess up countless times. He just waits for an invitation from you to begin a personal, life-changing relationship with Him. And in John 10:10, He promises what that decision will bring you. He says, "I've come to the world to give LIFE—abundant life!"

Awesome promise!

So who knows? This book might wind up becoming more to you than straight talk on loneliness and the times when God feels far away. I've prayed that somehow, some of my readers might sense Christ's love even as they browse through these pages. Why? Like I've said over and over, every human relationship will fall painfully short of meeting the deepest longings for intimacy buried inside you. Only through personal relationship with Jesus Christ can a true sense of purpose, unconditional love and guidance for the future be captured.

If you're interested in starting this incredible journey, think about praying something like this:

Jesus, I don't think I picked this book up by accident. I'm a million miles from being perfect, but people tell me that Your love is bigger than all the junk and mistakes in my life. Thanks for dying on the cross for me...what a gutsy, selfless act of friendship.

The simple prayer that changes EVERYTHING

So in simple, kid-like faith, I ask You to come into my life right now. I'm asking You, Jesus, to become my Best Friend, my Savior, and the Boss of my life. I can't promise You perfection from this point on, but You know my heart. I really do want an authentic, personal relationship with You. So according to what the Bible teaches, this simple but heartfelt action now makes me "Your kid." By faith in Your Word, I now choose to believe that I am a new person- from the inside out. Help me as I begin this exciting journey of being an authentic Christ-follower. I pray this in Jesus' Name. Amen.

I've prayed a prayer kind of like that with thousands of young adults and teenagers all over the globe. And believe me, it works! I promise. Even more strategic, let me say again that your personal relationship with Christ will become the single greatest relationship you can ever, ever cultivate. He alone can create the "Dream Relationship" that we all long about and fill the lonely places of your heart.

And that, my friend, is the most important UNCENSORED truth you'll receive in your entire lifetime.

Lovingly Honored to be in the Same "Family,"

Jeanne

If you prayed this prayer today and really meant it, please contact my publisher, HigherLife Development Services, on the Web at **www.ahigherlife.com** to receive a free gift to help in your new walk with Christ. If you'd rather, you may write them at...

HigherLife Development Services, Inc.

2342 Westminster Terrace

Oviedo, FL 32765

jeanne mayo's
youth**leader's**coach

www.youthleaderscoach.com

No one ever made it
to the big game
without a coach...
So why tackle youth
ministry without
one ?

coaching
Jeanne's most valuable tools for winning the game.
Monthly mentoring at its best

the vault
Free youth leadership coaching shared by Jeanne and
other premiere youth leaders from across the nation

resources
Every great team needs the right equipment to succeed

our forum
Interactive message board where youth leaders share
ideas and events that actually work

calendar
Jeanne speaks frequently across the nation and
internationally to large youth gatherings and youth
leadership forums. See when she is in your area

for more information call us @ 404.284.826?

ABOUT THE AUTHOR

Acclaimed by Ministries Today as "America's Number One Youth Pastor," Jeanne Mayo has thrown her heart and passion into youth ministry for nearly four decades. Her ministry DNA is reflected in her life mission statement: "The motivation and mentorship of Kamikaze Christianity into practicing and potential Kingdom champions."

The years have seen incredible results. In Nebraska, she multiplied a group of a few dozen students into hundreds. Then in Illinois, she was met by a group of 30 students that grew to nearly 1,000 and a Christian school of 1,400. While in California, she had the privilege of developing a group of 90 students into over 500 in only one year's time. Currently, she and her husband are leading an incredible team in Atlanta where amazing growth is happening once again.

Jeanne's successful ministry has placed her in high demand as a youth ministry and youth leadership communicator. She has criss-crossed the U.S. and the globe, speaking in countless venues to teenagers, college students as well as their leaders. Now one of her greatest joys during these travels is to re-connect with hundreds of her spiritual sons and daughters in fulltime ministry all over the world.

www.youthleaderscoach.com

In recent years, Jeanne founded *Youth Leader's Coach*, a non-profit organization that seeks, "To instruct, equip, inspire and encourage the youth pastors and youth leaders of this generation."

Through *Youth Leader's Coach*, Jeanne is now focusing on leaving a legacy for youth pastors and youth leaders of this generation. She is a coach, mentor and "Big Sis" to youth leaders across the country. Jeanne is also pouring her heart into creating resources designed specifically for those impacting the lives of teenagers. She is a regular columnist for *Group Magazine* and *Ministries Today*. She most recently authored the popular leadership book, *Thriving Youth Groups* and the first book in this series, *Uncensored: Dating, Friendship and Sex*.

In response to Jeanne's achievements in youth and young adult ministry, Oral Roberts University awarded her a Doctorate of Divinity. Jeanne also sponsors, through *Youth Leader's Coach*, her *National Youth Leaders' Conference*. This widely acclaimed event has become one of the largest gatherings of its kind, drawing thousands of youth pastors and leaders in 2005 as well as 2009.

Jeanne found her way to the cross as a young teenage woman. After college, she married her "hero," Pastor Sam Mayo, who has been the Senior Pastor at most places she served. Jeanne considers her most cherished accolade, however, to be that she is the proud mom of two adult sons, Josh and Justin. Jeanne's favorite quote comes from missionary Jim Elliot and contains the words that motivate her to live out her life mission ...

 "He is no fool who gives what he cannot keep to gain what he cannot lose."

To contact Jeanne Mayo,
please write to:

Youth Leader's Coach
P.O. Box 450309
Atlanta, Georgia 31145
Phone: 404.284.8262

Email: info@youthleaderscoach.com

Or visit her on the Web at:

www.youthleaderscoach.com